Kids You Ought to Know

By Courtney Granet Raff

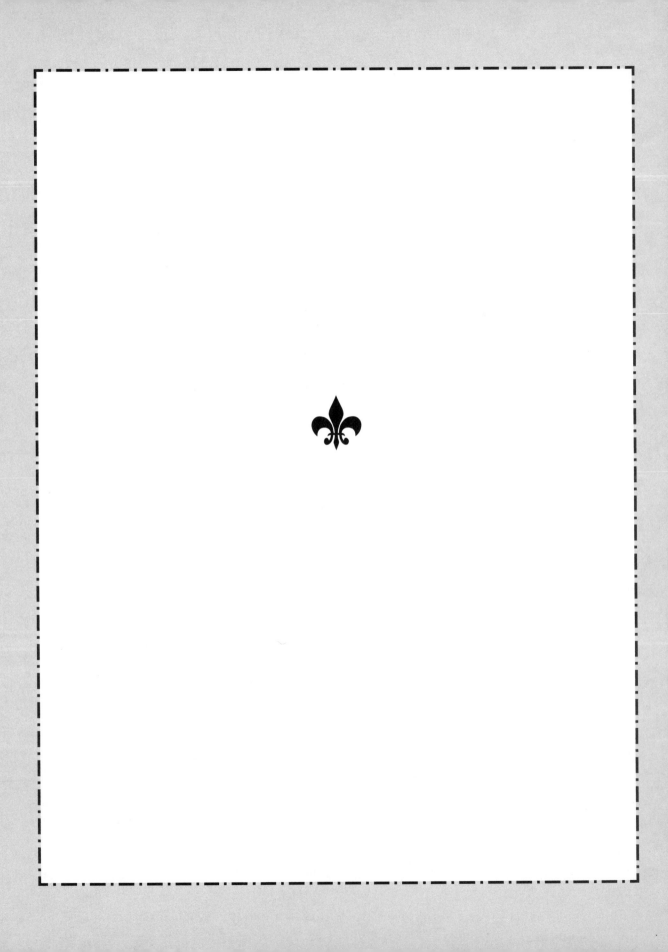

Contents

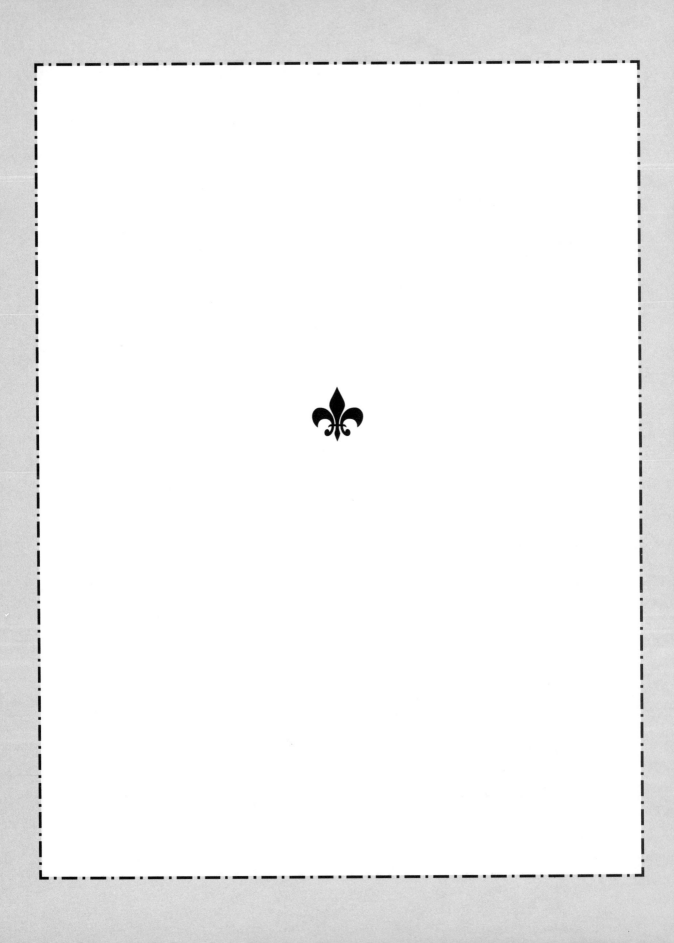

Introduction

What do you think of when you hear the word *hero?* Is it a person in a red cape swooping down from the top of a tall building? Perhaps you picture someone famous who you've read about. It could be a character with magical powers, or a relative, teacher, or friend.

There is no wrong answer. There are many kinds of heroes who possess traits like bravery, courage, intellect, kindness, or determination. Can you think of other heroic qualities?

Heroes are all different ages, races, genders, and more. Even the family dog can be a hero, warning its owners about uninvited guests. Some heroes fight for causes they feel strongly about, whether it is to save the earth or collect necessary items for those in need. Others overcome bad luck or difficulty and go on to accomplish great feats. A hero might react swiftly and unselfishly to a life-threatening event.

What do these different heroes have in common? They all have strength of character. They know what is right and wrong, and act properly. All heroes have made choices—based on their own personal beliefs—to do what needs to be done and "fix what is broken."

We all have the ability to be heroic. It is up to us to choose what we feel strongly about, set a goal, and take actions to reach that goal. Any step to make a positive difference is an important one.

Making a difference does not have to be as huge as the accomplishments of historical figures, such as Martin Luther King, Jr. who fought for civil rights, or Helen Keller, a blind and deaf girl who later became a writer, teacher, and activist. Making a positive difference by doing small things, like acts of kindness, makes you a hero, too.

Kids You Ought to Know will help you form your own definition of a hero, and perhaps inspire you to make a heroic effort, big or small, in your life. Just remember, kids can make a difference, too!

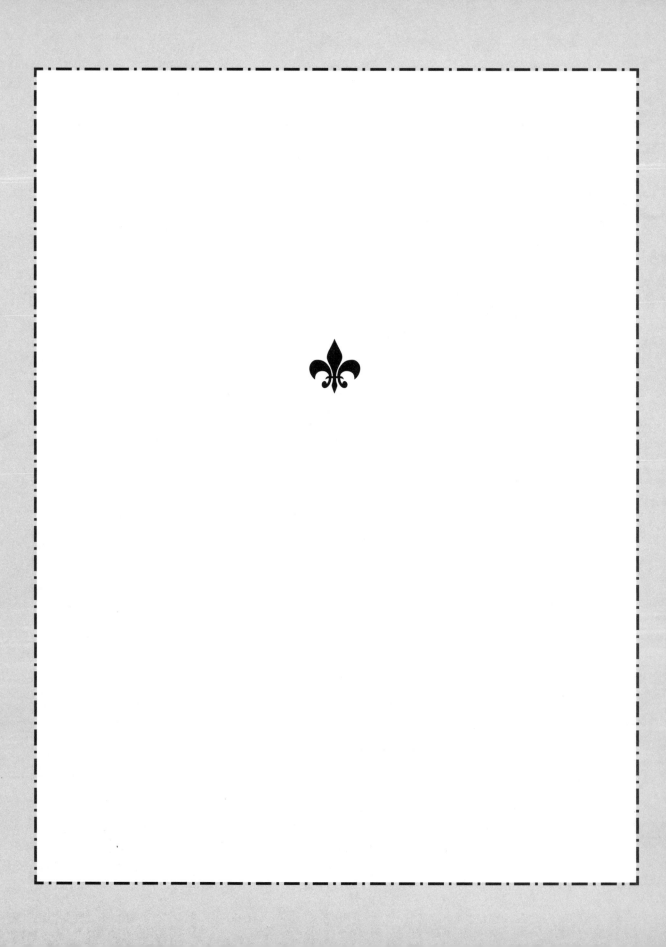

Annie Wignall

One cold January day, 11-year-old Annie Wignall from Iowa was doing her homework and waiting for her mother to come home from work. Annie's mother, Cathy, is a child abuse prevention educator for Jasper County. Cathy teaches preschool and elementary-aged children how to recognize, resist, and report abusive behavior. She has dedicated her life to kids by teaching them how to stay safe. Annie knows her mother's job is very important.

When Cathy arrived home that day, she was sad and upset because of what she had learned at a work meeting. Cathy told Annie that the meeting was about children who are taken away from their homes for various reasons. Some parents have died, so their kids need new caregivers. Other parents are unable to take care of their kids properly. Some homes are considered unsafe, and children need to be removed. Many kids in these situations are forced to leave their homes immediately, without any warning and with nothing but the clothes on their back. Then they're brought to unfamiliar foster homes and homeless shelters. Annie understood that these children are taken away for their safety, but she was upset about the hardship they must deal with as it happens.

That night, when Annie lay in bed, her mind was racing. How awful it must be to be taken away from your home, your caregivers, and your stuff, with nothing familiar or comforting to hold! A million plans were flying around in her brain. She knew that she had to do something to help comfort these children.

The participants at Cathy's meeting were asked to collect items like

shampoo, soap, and toothbrushes for these kids. Annie realized that such items are necessary but also knew that they wouldn't offer any emotional relief to these unsettled children. Annie thought these kids deserved things that would provide comfort to them as well. A few of her ideas included books, toys, and stuffed animals. Annie wanted to give these children a bag that included necessary items as well as some familiar items they'd cherish.

She believed the new things she would collect should be presented as a gift to the children, and not just thrown together in a paper bag. Annie wanted the bag to be sewn out of fabric, something special that they could hold on to forever. She also wanted the items to be carefully and lovingly placed inside the bag. Annie explained, "I want these kids to know that someone cares about them and wants them to be happy." So before she fell asleep, Annie had her plan. Care Bags was born!

Before Annie got her plan off the ground, she needed to make sure that agencies that serve homeless and needy children would be interested in her idea. So she called two local agencies and both were thrilled with her plan, offering to hand out the Care Bags to the kids they provided aid to.

Annie quickly took action. The first thing she did was to contact a group of women from northern Iowa that, she'd heard, liked to sew for special causes. This group was more than happy to help. In fact, these women sewed and donated all the bags for an entire first year.

Then Annie wrote a list of necessary, safe, and fun items to be put into the bags, making sure to include items that fit the needs of different age groups. She had to figure out how to get the large number of new items needed. She decided to ask businesses to make donations. Annie wrote a letter explaining her cause and met with managers of local businesses. These businesses all agreed to donate to Care Bags.

Annie successfully completed the hardest parts of her project, taking care of all the necessary details. Then she used her creative skills to write a poem with her mother, a color-coded poem that would be attached to every Care Bag. Pink paper was used for babies and toddlers, blue for 3 to 12-year-olds, and yellow for 13 to 18-year-olds.

> *This little bag was made*
> *especially for you,*
> *to say I think you're special*
> *and I care about you too.*
>
> *Inside you'll find a bunch of things*
> *like toothpaste, soap, or toy,*
> *I collected all this stuff for you*
> *to fill your heart with joy.*
>
> *I hope this makes you happy*
> *today and every day,*
> *and remember someone loves you*
> *in a very special way.*

By the end of the first year, the project had really grown. Care Bags were given to children in foster care, to homeless or badly treated children, or to any child in need. Care Bags organization was getting more recognition and as a result, many more agencies were requesting its services. Annie needed more sewn bags and donations to keep up with the demand, so she recruited friends, neighbors, and school and community members to sew. She sent out newsletters and spoke to service clubs, churches, and youth and senior-citizens groups, asking for their help. Care Bags also posted information on volunteer websites to reach as many people as possible throughout the country. A computer expert volunteered to design a website for her project, which helped get the word out to people all over the world.

Annie's small community project that started out of her home has grown into a charitable, nonprofit organization. With the help and kindness of others, and support from thousands of people and businesses all over the country, Annie and her volunteers (ages 2–92!) fill over 100 Care Bags each month at the Care Bags headquarters. By working with many American and international agencies who hand-deliver the bags, Annie's organization has been able to provide Care Bags to more than 7,000 needy children all over the world—most recently to young victims of Hurricane Katrina. Although Annie has gotten a great deal of attention for her work—including meeting President Bush—it's not attention she craves. She says, "seeing the smiles on the faces of the beautiful kids I help is the best reward I will ever get."

Among the lessons that Annie has learned through her work with Care Bags is the value of family. She is thankful for her family's support and for her good life. Annie has also learned how powerful a group of people can become when they gather together for a good cause.

Annie feels that people of all ages can help by donating time, items, and money or by sewing bags, bibs, and blankets. She urges kids and adults to start similar projects in their own community so that more children in need will feel cared for. A free "starter kit" is available through her website: **www.carebags4kids.org**.

Today Annie remains quite busy! After all, she's the founder, director, and president of the Care Bags Foundation. But this teenager's life is full of many other things, too. Annie likes school. She feels that she has great teachers and many friends. Annie is active with her school soccer team, band, drama group, and chorus.

Because Annie enjoys being around kids, she babysits and performs for children in her spare time. Annie performs with two community service groups. One is called Happy Bear, which puts on a child abuse prevention play for kids. The other is called New Kids on the Block, which puts on a puppet show that teaches kids to accept disabilities. Annie is getting lots of good practice with kids to fulfill her dream of becoming a kindergarten teacher.

Annie Wignall is just a regular person who has great compassion, especially for kids who are forced into scary, lonely situations. Instead of simply recognizing the problem, she took the next step and did something about it. She hopes kids will get involved in whatever they feel strongly about. "Whatever it is, find something you care about and like to do, and take action....You don't have to take big steps or do anything huge.... Smile at a stranger, clean up your neighborhood.... Even though we're young, we can make a difference in the world by the little things we do."

Annie Wignall
Founder of Care Bags Foundation

Allison Cartwright

*A*llison Cartwright is very close to her mother. One day in early spring, eight-year-old Allison went with her mom to a blood drive and watched her donate blood. Allison was curious why her mom's blood bag was given a special tag, and found out that the tag indicated that this blood supply was to be set aside for people who have a disease called *sickle cell anemia*.

Allison's mom had requested the special tag, and Allison wanted to know why. Her mother arranged for Allison to take a tour of the Hematology Department at a nearby children's hospital. She saw children

with sickle cell anemia and learned that such children desperately need blood transfusions. Allison decided that she wanted to help.

Sickle cell anemia is a disease of the red blood cells that affects mainly (but not only) black people. The job of the red blood cells is to carry oxygen throughout the body. Normal, healthy red blood cells are smooth and doughnut-shaped and can easily latch onto oxygen cells and carry the oxygen throughout

the body. But people with sickle cell anemia have red blood cells that are stiff and become curved, which makes it difficult for the cells to hold onto the oxygen. These deformed red blood cells also become trapped in the body's small blood vessels and block them.

In a healthy individual, blood normally flows freely through these small blood vessels to carry healthy red blood cells with oxygen throughout the body. But because people with sickle cell anemia have less oxygen for their bodies, and the transportation of the available oxygen becomes less efficient, they have difficulty getting oxygen to all parts of their bodies. This causes pain and eventually damages organs. Those who have this disease often get very sick and suffer from strokes, heart attacks, and kidney problems. They typically don't live past the age of about 40.

Allison also learned that while only five percent of the United States' population gives blood, about 96 percent of the population will need it at some point (mostly for reasons other than sickle cell anemia). At certain times, kids with sickle cell anemia need many units of blood, but since Allison was too young and too small to give blood herself (you have to be at least 17 years old and weigh at least 110 pounds), she needed to find other ways to help.

Allison has discovered a variety of ways to reach as many people as possible. One way she does this is by spending much of her free time reminding people to give blood. For example, Allison and her mom sometimes spend an entire afternoon in the mall, handing out information and reminder magnets. They make the magnets on their home computer, printing them out on special magnet paper. Allison says, "I figure if they have a magnet, they will put it on their refrigerator so that they can remind themselves to give." Since Allison's main focus is to help kids with sickle cell anemia, she frequently approaches African Americans because their blood is the best match. As she encourages people to give blood, she assures them that it's not painful. Allison explains that they'll "only feel a slight pinch."

In addition to Allison's concern for kids with sickle cell anemia, she has other interests. She plays soccer and basketball, takes hip-hop dance lessons, plays the cello, and likes hanging out with her dog, Pepper. Allison also enjoys shopping at the mall and checking out the latest styles. Allison hopes one day to live in Paris and to design clothes.

Allison's work for sickle cell anemia sufferers has made a big difference. She figured out a way to help and did not get discouraged, even though she was too young to give blood. Allison feels that all kids can make an impact, and she has some advice for kids who want to help. If they're too young to give blood themselves, kids can encourage adults they know to donate. They may choose to do this by sharing with adults a printout of the information found on **http://www.pleasegiveblood.org/**. Getting involved can take some time and effort, but Allison feels it's all worth it. She adds, "Even though it might be hard, if you break it down into small steps, it can be done."

Joshua & Christopher Ballard

*I*t is great to have one amazing kid in a family, but having two is remarkable! Fourteen-year-old Joshua Ballard and 16-year-old Christopher Ballard are brothers who live in California. These boys are achieving a great deal in their young lives. Joshua and Christopher share some similar talents, yet these brothers have independently developed their unique abilities.

Both boys were home-schooled from kindergarten until sixth grade. Joshua and Christopher know the importance of an education. But they also know it's necessary to explore all sorts of activities outside the classroom. It is these outside experiences that have played a big part in leading the Ballard brothers toward pursuing their interests and achieving their goals.

JOSHUA

Joshua explains that ever since he was a toddler, he has always been drawn to computers and high-tech equipment. When he was ten years old, he wanted to pursue his interest in technology. Joshua reports, "Since my family [was] on a tight budget, I decided to create my own business so I could afford high-tech equipment." He started a company called Ballard International, where he's the president and CEO.

Joshua's company allows him to capitalize on his skills and interests. He offers the public his services as a motivational public speaker, photographer, website developer, and graphic artist. Joshua explains, "As the owner of my own business, I have the opportunity to do what I enjoy, work at my own leisure, meet many friends, and earn money at the same time. With the money that I earn, I can purchase expensive computer equipment…[which will] help to enhance the quality of the service that my company provides."

Joshua's company gave him so much satisfaction that he wanted to show others how to turn their talents and experiences into businesses that would earn them money. Joshua designed a business course for kids

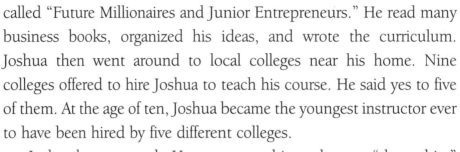

called "Future Millionaires and Junior Entrepreneurs." He read many business books, organized his ideas, and wrote the curriculum. Joshua then went around to local colleges near his home. Nine colleges offered to hire Joshua to teach his course. He said yes to five of them. At the age of ten, Joshua became the youngest instructor ever to have been hired by five different colleges.

Joshua loves to teach. He encourages his students to "dream big." He tells them, "If life gives you lemons, make delicious lemonade!" Once his students graduate, he feels he has attained his goal. Joshua explains, "I am happy that they, too, are young entrepreneurs who earn money doing what they enjoy the most." Joshua remains friendly with many of his students.

Ballard International continues to have a good reputation and is developing a steady increase of clients. The company has received a lot of media coverage in the United States and around the world. Throughout the past few years, Joshua has gained a great deal of practice and recognition as a public speaker through his involvement in media events, through teaching, and by guest speaking at functions such as the International Children's Film Festival and the National Coalition for Empowering Youth Entrepreneurs. A naturally outgoing and friendly individual, he enjoys public speaking and hopes to make motivational speaking a large part of his future career.

Joshua puts a lot of thought into his future. At this point he wants his public-speaking career to focus on kids. He wants to help them recognize and use their talents. In order to do this, Joshua would like one day to host his own television talk show. In this way he could spotlight youth all over the United States who are accomplishing great things and becoming outstanding citizens. Joshua could then motivate and teach his viewers how to use their abilities to do meaningful things in their own lives.

CHRISTOPHER

Christopher Ballard, who is two years older than his brother, Joshua, has also had his share of the spotlight. Christopher is an award-winning violinist, pianist, and composer. He describes himself as a perfectionist who practices the violin and piano for several hours a day.

Even as a toddler he enjoyed attending concerts with his family. "While listening to the orchestra, I was always captivated by the sound of the violin. In fact, it almost seemed to me that the violin was calling my name. When I received my first toy violin, I knew [this instrument] was meant for me." Christopher began violin lessons at age six, and by age seven, he began piano lessons.

In addition, Christopher focused on chess, another one of his many interests. Christopher was so good at chess that at age seven, he set a chess tournament record in Beverly Hills. He was the first player to win all of his games in his first competition. Since then he has won many other trophies in Scholastic Chess Championships.

When Christopher was seven, he began to share his gift of music with the public. He performed for hundreds of different audiences, from national conventions to fund-raising events.

Christopher found out that there was much more to performing than simply playing the instrument he loved. He had to play on stage in front of huge audiences and also had to respond publicly to awards that were presented to him and to the praise he received. Today Christopher is used to handling himself in public and does so very well, but it wasn't always this way. When he first began to perform, Christopher was extremely shy and didn't feel comfortable playing or speaking in front of an audience. He had to overcome this problem before he could deal with the constant public attention that followed him.

To help him become more confident on stage and in the spotlight, Christopher's parents encouraged him to try many different social activities, such as tae kwon do, music competitions, and musical theater.

While overcoming his shyness, Christopher was also becoming aware of how inspiring he was—helping others to overcome their hurdles and to do their best. He was amazed at the positive influence a person can have on others. Christopher believes that any problem can be solved and anything can be achieved when an individual recognizes his or her strengths and weaknesses, hopes and dreams, and can work well with others.

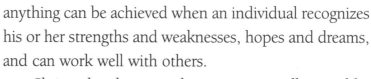

Christopher has now become an excellent public speaker. During his musical performances, he focuses on his love of music instead of his fear of the audience. His breathtaking music and confident stage presence continue to result in great performances and honors.

The two performances he's proudest of were both when he was 13 years old. Christopher had a solo violin performance at the Classical Grammy Awards ceremony. He received a standing ovation after he finished playing. But nothing made him feel prouder than when he was performing at President George W. Bush's first inauguration, where he played solo violin before thousands of people, including the millions who watched the program on television. He received a standing ovation for his performance, and his family was invited to attend a private luncheon at the White House.

Christopher has set many goals. He plans to study law and enter the world of politics, hoping one day to become the President of the United States. And because Christopher is so passionate about the importance of education, he hopes to be able to educate children all over the world. Christopher feels, "When children are exposed to cultures other than their own…it promotes harmony."

Christopher believes reading is one of the best ways to become educated. He is usually the first person in the family to get up in the morning and the last to go to sleep at night so he can read. He even grabs some extra time to read—in the middle of the night! Christopher believes that *readers* are *leaders*. He encourages others to read biographies and autobiographies of remarkable people. By doing so kids will realize that everyone—even the most successful people—have ups and downs in their lives, as well as strengths and weaknesses. That knowledge will help kids become more accepting of themselves and their lives. Christopher also believes that readers can imitate the successes and avoid the mistakes of the famous people they read about.

• • • • •

Joshua and Christopher have been separately recognized for their many personal successes. They have also experienced some of the same media attention. The following are only a few that both boys share:

- Joshua, some of Joshua's students, and Christopher were featured on NBC's *The John Walsh Show*. The program was entitled "Teens Striking It Rich: Young Entrepreneurs."
- Channel 5 (Fox) celebrated Joshua's accomplishments by featuring him on "Making It." Channel 5 celebrated Christopher's accomplishments by featuring him as one of the "Unsung Heroes" in a television documentary.
- Joshua and Christopher appeared together on the "Hour of Power" and on *The Montel Williams Show*.

Although the Ballard boys are busy with all of their activities and performances, they feel that they are "normal" kids. For fun, Joshua enjoys playing golf, chess, and sailing with friends. Christopher likes hanging out with his friends and going to the movies and arcades. Both boys get a great deal of love, support, and guidance from their parents and from each other. They are also very passionate about their religious faith.

The Ballard brothers are like sponges, soaking up all of life's experiences. Their knowledge comes from books, school, current events, and the media. They continue to learn how to use their extraordinary gifts to help change the world for the better. The Ballards hope they can inspire others to pursue new experiences and find hidden strengths.

Carlos Pena

On the day 12-year-old Carlos Pena of Houston, Texas, came up with the idea for his great invention, he had no thoughts of winning a prize or getting any recognition. He was simply spending the day in his quiet neighborhood helping his father work on cars, and he just wanted to make his dad's life a little bit easier.

Carlos's father is a car mechanic, which is very often complicated work. Carlos has his father's knack for fixing things. He loves taking things apart and seeing how they work.

One day Carlos noticed his father using a tool that looked similar to an antenna. It was a long, skinny magnet used to pick up little pieces of

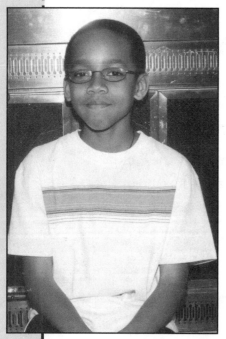

metal, like screws and nails. This instrument could pick up only one object at a time. As he watched his father work, it occurred to Carlos that this tool could be made more efficient by strengthening its magnetism so it could pick up several things at once.

Carlos began to put together a prototype, or sample, of an improved tool. Carlos found the process of making the prototype to be more difficult than he had expected and became very frustrated at times. But he didn't give up. He initially wanted the entire instrument to be made out of metal, but he couldn't find anything the right size. He settled on Styrofoam. Then he attached small magnets, large heavy-duty ones, and an extendable mirror. His mother took him shopping for materials. And his dad helped him use heavy-duty equipment to cut the materials. Carlos pressed on, working each day for several weeks to get his invention to look exactly the way he wanted. Part of the challenge was cutting the Styrofoam to look like a hand. This was important because Carlos decided to name his invention "A Helping Hand."

When Carlos was finished with his "helping hand," his science teacher, Ms. Bobineax, entered it into the Craftsman/NSTA (National Science Teachers Association) Young Inventors Award Program. Carlos was one of the winners in this national contest. This gave him the opportunity to travel to California and share his work nationally on television on *The Tonight Show with Jay Leno* and *The Ellen DeGeneres Show*. Carlos happily reported, "The whole experience has been really fun, and I hope to do more fun things and meet new people." His family and friends now call him "the inventor." He has other inventions in the works, but he's keeping them secret for now. Carlos plans to enter them into the Craftsman/NSTA Young Inventors Award Program contest for the next three years until he will be past the grade limit for entries.

This young inventor has recently applied his talent to Odyssey of the Mind, an international educational program that challenges students from kindergarten through college to use their bright minds and skills to solve problems. Each team has several problems to solve, and Carlos's team made it to the state level and placed third. Carlos has other interests as well, including music. He plays cello and piano.

Carlos is very close to his family, including his parents and two sisters. He believes that "having family time is really cool." He especially likes Saturdays when his family goes to church together. Carlos feels very thankful for his parents, who support him in many ways. "They do things like help me with my projects for school and take me to all my after-school activities." And he tries to help them out whenever he can, too.

It was Carlos's kind heart, hard work, and determination that set him on the road to this inventing adventure. In the end it is his family's love and support for one another that helps him reap such great rewards.

Bobby Anderson

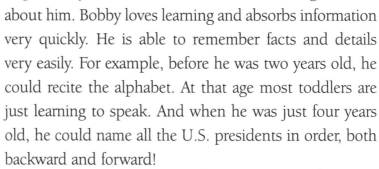

*A*bout 40 miles outside of Chicago, you might find 11-year-old Bobby Anderson speaking Chinese with his mother or speaking English with his friends. He could be doing skateboard tricks, practicing the trumpet, painting pictures of plum blossoms, or walking his dog, Tuni. Bobby's got a lot of interesting things going on in his life.

Even when Bobby was very young, he had a rare ability for learning things quickly. People always knew that there was something unusual about him. Bobby loves learning and absorbs information very quickly. He is able to remember facts and details very easily. For example, before he was two years old, he could recite the alphabet. At that age most toddlers are just learning to speak. And when he was just four years old, he could name all the U.S. presidents in order, both backward and forward!

Since Bobby's mother, Rita, is Chinese, and his father, Keith, is American, Bobby decided that he wanted to learn both English and Chinese. So of course he mastered both languages. At age five, Bobby sang the Chinese national anthem at the retirement party for the Chinese Consul General in Chicago, an important government official. And then at age six, he sang the U.S. national anthem at a minor league baseball game.

At age seven, Bobby memorized the names of all the provinces of China. At age eight, he won third prize in a piano competition, playing "Für Elise," a famous piece by Beethoven. Bobby achieved the rank of deputy black belt in tae kwon do. At age nine, he completed a math course called pre-algebra. And at age ten, he took an algebra course that is normally taken by freshmen in high school! His constant thirst for knowledge was all self-motivated.

Now Bobby gets up at 5:30 A.M. to go to the University of Chicago Laboratory School, which is a private school on the university's campus. Bobby likes his school and his "really great teachers who are nice and teach well." He enjoys his classes in computers, library, and physical education. He also likes writer's workshop, band, and field trips—especially to museums and parks. Bobby enjoys his free time, too, when he can hang out, play, and explore with his friends.

Bobby's school week has one extra day—it goes from Monday through Saturday. Bobby's parents decided that it was important for him to learn more about Chinese language and culture. So on Saturdays, from 11:00 A.M. to 4:00 P.M., Bobby goes to a special Chinese school called the Xilin Academy. There he learns to speak, read, and write both Mandarin and Cantonese, two of the major dialects of China. He does advanced math work and even practices Ping-Pong, a very popular sport in both China and America. Bobby has been named a top student of Xilin Academy.

One of his favorite activities at Saturday school is dance. He is a member of the White Rabbits Dance Troupe. The group performs dances that are mostly traditional folk dances but with many modern steps added. Bobby's current favorite is "Young Mongolian Riders," a dance in which the kids act out, in dance form, riding horses across the plains.

When Bobby was nine years old, his hard work in his dance group brought him an interesting opportunity. The White Rabbits Dance Troupe traveled to China (near Beijing) and got to perform in the Tianjin Children's Art Festival. Bobby describes the festival as "a very spectacular show that lasted seven days and involved kids from more than 35 countries, and all the provinces of China."

Aside from participating in the festival, Bobby had a week to explore China as a tourist. He loved walking around the cities of China and talking to people, which was especially fun since he speaks both Mandarin and Cantonese. Bobby joined his friends in "Climb the Great Wall" competition, finishing with a second-place trophy, behind Puerto Rico. He also had fun visiting the museums, an old army fort, and discovering Beijing's Forbidden City, which lies in the center of Beijing and is the world's largest palace complex, surrounded by a deep moat and a high wall.

Bobby absorbs a great deal from all of his experiences. He continues to explore different activities and learn new skills, such as guitar, camping, and skiing. He has also studied brush painting with the master artist Andy Chan and has become expert at this skill. He plans to start his own company, dealing mostly in the sale of original Chinese calligraphy and

painting. Bobby was a featured guest at the 2005 inaugural gala of the Chicago Guangzhou Association. He gave a speech in four languages (English, Cantonese, Mandarin, and Spanish) and raffled off three of his paintings.

Bobby has established both short-term and long-term goals for himself. He plans to continue working hard and hopes to get excellent grades in order to fulfill his dream of going to Harvard. He also has a deal with his father. If Bobby gets all A's, his father promises to dye his hair green and go to work that way. Bobby thinks that would be really funny looking!

The multitalented Bobby wants to learn how to snowboard. He also ... Microsoft. In addition, Bobby ... do stunt work.

Ashley Torres

The first time Ashley Torres saw a Bruce Lee movie, she couldn't take her eyes off the screen. Bruce Lee was a master of martial arts, which are different styles or skills of self-defense. These sports were originally used for fighting, and some styles include judo and karate. But Bruce Lee's style as a martial artist was like no other—he combined many different styles to develop his own. Ashley was impressed by his smooth, beautiful, and powerful dance-like movements, as well as his focus, control, and discipline. She knew she wanted to learn martial arts.

It has been a few years since Ashley saw that Bruce Lee movie. She has since been practicing three to four times a week with her karate instructors, Joshua David Gonzalez, Deshi Dushan DuBose, and Sensei Bryan Gotthoffer. She also practices with her stepfather, Louis Velazquez, when she is at home. Lou Velazquez is president of Karate Kidz Online, the largest martial arts website in the world, dedicated to all youth involved in martial arts. He explains that it was Ashley who inspired him to use this website (**www.karatekidzonline.com**) as a tool to help kids around the world. "She is someone that other children can look up to. In this day and age, the kids need to know that they can do better for themselves beyond what they see on the street corner." Lou explains that martial arts is a great vehicle for kids to empower themselves and reach their potential through physical, mental, and spiritual training.

Ashley is accomplishing her goals. She has moved up many levels since she first started. In the karate studio, stripes are based on attendance and the belt color is based on skill level. She successfully competes against her peers, having earned first-place trophies in sparring and forms. Ashley is one of the few girls in her karate class. It does not bother her that she is outnumbered by boys—Ashley believes more girls should take self-defense classes so they can learn to protect themselves.

Ashley feels great passion for more than just throwing punches in her karate class. In fact, she is grateful for everything that she has in her life now. Ashley's life has not always been easy. She has had to deal with difficult times, including the deaths of her grandmother and father. In 2001 her apartment caught on fire, and she and her mother barely escaped. Luckily they were unharmed, but they had to pack up their belongings and leave their home.

For a little while, Ashley and her mom, Allison, moved in with Ashley's aunt and uncle. Because Allison had to work long hours, she wanted Ashley to be independent and to be able to protect herself. Ashley and Allison spoke about the possibility of martial arts, but classes were too expensive at the time.

When Ashley was five, things improved. Allison met Louis Velazquez, and Ashley and Lou got along very well. Ashley mentioned to Lou how much she enjoyed that Bruce Lee movie and that she was interested in

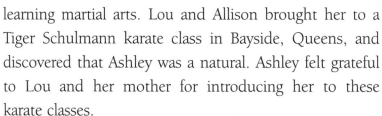

learning martial arts. Lou and Allison brought her to a Tiger Schulmann karate class in Bayside, Queens, and discovered that Ashley was a natural. Ashley felt grateful to Lou and her mother for introducing her to these karate classes.

As Valentine's Day of that year approached, Ashley decided to take another matter into her own hands. She suggested that Lou "get on one knee with a ring and flowers" and ask her mother to marry him. This way, Ashley pointed out, Lou could become her father. Lou took Ashley's suggestion, Allison said yes, and the couple married in 2001.

Lou adopted Ashley soon after. Ashley explains that her new dad watches movies with her, including a lot of martial arts and wrestling videos. Lou used to be a professional wrestler, and Ashley is very interested in watching wrestling to learn more about it.

Ashley enjoys her life and realizes how lucky she is to have such caring parents who support her. "My mom and dad inspire me because they take the time to give me so many examples of the right things to do in life so that when I grow up I will be a good person."

Indeed, Ashley has a big heart and derives true joy from helping people. She explains, "I am so happy that being in karate lets me help other kids and maybe can let them know that they are special, too. All that they need to do is work hard, be a good person, help other people, and set a good example for others."

Ashley enjoys seeing others around her succeed at something that they had struggled with, such as doing well on a difficult test. Those who help others in need also impress her.

Both children and adults are inspired by Ashley—the small girl with great physical and mental strength. Ashley's focus and kind heart have helped her survive difficult times, make smart choices, and surround herself with a lot of love and happiness in her life.

If Ashley could change anything about the world it would be "…that so many people wouldn't be sick and they could be healthy and happy in life." Maybe one day she will contribute to that dream. After all, one of the things that Ashley wants to be when she grows up is a doctor. She is also thinking about modeling. Ashley says that she will work hard to develop her skills.

There is no doubt that Ashley's training has helped her focus on accomplishing her goals. Ashley was selected Karate Kidz Online Student of the Month for October 2002, Amazing Kids! Kid of the Month for November 2002, Kids Hall of Fame in December 2002, and was chosen as a 2005 National American Miss New York State finalist.

She hopes to live her life to the fullest and touch many lives along the way. Ashley advises, "Always remember that there are good things out there for you. Just look around."

Life
By Ashley Torres

Life is a breathtaking time,
Having proms, marriages, and educating children
Meeting people, Celebrities and Masters
That you thought that you would never see
Wonder about things you thought
You would never wonder about
Making pictures in your mind, being an artist
Whose drawings are in museums
Being the best person that you can be.

Evan Kui

Fifteen-year-old Evan Kui has liked music since he was a baby. When he was two years old, he started singing a song that he had heard on television, even before he was really speaking! It was as if music were his primary language. His mother knew then that he had a real talent. When Evan was five, he started playing the piano. Within five minutes he played his first scale, and ever since then he's been "tickling the ivories."

Evan explains that music has always come naturally to him. He says "[I got] a feeling in my head when I was playing the piano…it's like I already knew how to read the notes when I never saw them before." Even now when he plays, his natural talent "just flows." He explains that this happens especially when he reaches the most moving part of a song, where he can "play beyond belief."

Evan is seriously committed to playing the piano. He practices every weekday for at least three hours after school, and on weekends from 11:00 A.M. to 3:00 P.M. Evan admits that his long practice schedule is difficult, but he feels it's rewarding. He says, "When you enjoy something, you can play for an eternity," and adds, "Whether I am sad or happy when I play, I always get inspired to play my best." Even during difficult times, Evan feels much happier when playing the piano.

Evan has had some excellent musical help along the way, including three special music teachers. His first piano teacher was Fugen Wei, a once renowned pianist in Shanghai. Fugen Wei helped Evan mostly with his stage presence and performance. Evan won many competitions under Fugen Wei's guidance. Evan's piano instructor now is Noune Grigorian, a professor from Moscow, who is also a talented pianist. She gives Evan his weekly lessons. In addition to piano, Evan also plays the tenor saxophone. He is taught by his school band teacher, Kim Monroe. Evan describes her as an "excellent instructor who plays lots of instruments, her favorite being the bassoon."

Evan participates in competitions about five times a year. Even though he has won a number of them, competitions still make him nervous. He feels a lot of pressure when "uncountable eyes" are staring at him. But once he starts playing, he focuses and gets absorbed in the music that he's making. The feeling he gets when he's finished and hears "a rain of applause" is "indescribable." That ending moment is very rewarding and makes it worth all the stress.

One of Evan's most vivid music memories was in 2000, at the Old Dominion University Department of Music, Classical Period Piano Competition. It was a tough competition. There were many accomplished young pianists, competing from around the country. Evan felt that he played well but not his very best, and he was doubtful whether he would win first or even second place. But he was proven wrong. He won first prize and was so excited that he described it to be like "fireworks…blowing up in my mind!"

In addition to winning first prize in 2000, Evan has received many other awards and a lot of recognition for his talent. Just to name a few, Evan won first place at Brooklyn Arts Council Piano Competition in 1999 and 2000, and second place in 2001. In 2000 Evan won first place in the New York Music Competition at Carnegie Hall, a famous concert hall in the heart of New York City. He feels that his skills increase every year that he plays. As he wins more awards, Evan is getting more confident and hopes that his confidence will someday "diminish [his] nervousness."

Besides playing the piano, Evan likes school, especially his teachers and friends. He considers his friends to be "his life" and feels that these friendships have helped him through many difficult situations.

Evan also enjoys sports, especially handball, which he wishes were a more popular sport. He enjoys the fast pace and action of hockey and really likes the feeling when he scores a goal and his teammates and the crowds "go crazy."

Despite his busy schedule, playing the piano is still Evan's favorite activity. He plans to continue playing in competitions. Evan feels that if he continues to win awards, he will one day become a famous pianist, recognized around the world. He's well on his way.

Evan finds enormous satisfaction in making an audience beam with happiness as they listen to his music, because it soothes their minds and warms their hearts. But most importantly, Evan realizes that although he has a very special musical gift, it is his gift of close friends that makes life worthwhile.

Iqbal Masih

*I*magine yourself at age five. Think about what you were doing. You might have been home, spending time with your family. Maybe you were in school, learning how to read and write from your teacher. You might have been eating a meal to help you grow healthy and strong. Maybe you were sick and visiting your doctor. Or you might have been playing and having fun.

Did you feel lucky to do these activities, or did you just think that was what all kids did? You may not realize it, but each of these basic activities is considered a "right" of every American child. All these rights make up children's rights laws and are protected and enforced by the United States government. No one can take away these rights.

Millions of children between the ages of four and 14, who live in other parts of the world, are not as lucky as American children because they don't have basic human rights. Some of these children have rights but do not have a government that will enforce these rights, so their rights are ignored. Therefore, the most basic childhood activities, or rights— playing, eating healthy meals, seeing a doctor, going to school—are not available to them. Sadly, many of these children stay very busy without such activities because they are forced into child labor.

Child labor requires children to spend their days working in unhealthy and abusive conditions. They are also kept from getting an education. Child labor is against the law in most parts of the world, but breaking this law is very common. Becoming enslaved to their jobs and their "masters" is the only childhood most of these children know.

In some countries, many factory owners take advantage of poor families who have no other choice but to sell their children into labor in exchange for a loan. The child becomes prisoner to the factory and its owners. Iqbal Masih was one of these children.

In 1986 four-year-old Iqbal was living in a small, quiet village in eastern Pakistan. Iqbal's family was very poor and lived in a tiny, two-room house made of clay. Iqbal's older sisters looked after him while their mother worked as a house cleaner to support the family. Iqbal's father had left them.

During this difficult time, Iqbal's older brother was getting married. In Pakistan, weddings are very important and meaningful celebrations. Even poor families must find a way to make a wedding celebration. Iqbal's father (although he had left his family), realized his responsibility and made a deal with the owner of a local carpet factory. In exchange for a loan of 600 rupees (about $12), he agreed to send his son, Iqbal, to work. Iqbal would stay in the factory and weave carpets until he earned enough money to pay off his father's debt. The responsibility to pay for the wedding was dumped on four-year-old Iqbal! The family at the time was also too poor to care for Iqbal, so with a handshake, young Iqbal went to work for the factory.

Six mornings a week, Iqbal was picked up at around 4:00 AM. He would then spend the next 12 to 14 hours of his day, for the next six years, in the same factory, squatting in front of a loom weaving carpets. He was often chained to this loom, so he could hardly move. The conditions in the factory were awful. The room Iqbal worked in was cramped, hot, and dusty, with no fresh air and very little light. His job, along with that of thousands of other children, was to tie knots to create colorful and detailed oriental rugs. Children were assigned the specific task of tying knots because they have more dexterity with their small fingers than an adult would have, enabling them to make tiny and intricate knots. Tying knot after knot, day after day, year after year, was torture. Iqbal felt scared, lonely, and exhausted.

A strict carpet master was always watching the young workers. Iqbal was not allowed to talk to the other children working near him.

If Iqbal was distracted or made a mistake, he was yelled at and beaten. If Iqbal accidentally cut himself with the sharp weaver's knife, the carpet master would pour hot oil on his cut to seal it. This was to keep Iqbal's blood from getting on the carpets. This happened to Iqbal many times.

Iqbal and his fellow workers had a short lunch break each day. They were given a tiny amount of food, usually rice. These children were almost always starving and exhausted. They were often too tired to play on their days off and instead just rested their weary bodies.

The work took a toll on Iqbal's malnourished body. After spending years doing the exact same job in the identical position, Iqbal's body became deformed. His back grew curved and his hands became twisted, scarred, and calloused. Day after day he inhaled filthy air, so he also developed breathing problems. Many children suffered from the same kind of physical problems as Iqbal. Half of the Pakistani children in bonded labor died by the age of 12 from what is known as captive-child syndrome.

Even though Iqbal was living like a prisoner, his spirit was not crushed as his delicate fingers were. There came a point, after working so hard and under such bad conditions for so long, that Iqbal could no longer keep silent. He talked back to the carpet master, stuck up for his friends, and even refused to work. A few times, Iqbal tried to sneak out of the factory. Usually his failed attempts were met with punishment in the form of beating, scolding, and fines.

One day in 1992, Iqbal successfully escaped from the factory. As he got beyond the factory's jail-like high walls, Iqbal was finally on his way to discover freedom.

Iqbal found himself drawn to a crowd in the village square. The young boy crouched in a corner, fearful of being caught, but he was very interested in what had caused all the excitement around him. A man was giving a lively speech, and hundreds of people were cheering. The man speaking was Ehsan Ulla Khan, founder of the BLLF, or Bonded Labor Liberation Front. The BLLF was an organization that helped to free children like Iqbal from bonded labor. Ehsan spoke of the rights of child laborers and said that bonded labor was illegal in Pakistan. Iqbal could not believe his ears! After years of suffering, he felt hope and joy. Iqbal learned that he should be free!

After Ehsan completed his speech, he noticed small, shy Iqbal hiding in the corner. Ehsan went over to Iqbal, introduced himself, and asked Iqbal to speak in public about his experiences at the factory. Iqbal was hesitant at first, but then he gathered his courage and gave an eloquent speech about the factory's horrendous conditions and his cruel treatment there. From that moment on, Ehsan became Iqbal's friend and father figure.

Ehsan helped Iqbal find a BLLF lawyer to write him a "freedom" letter. Shortly after, armed with his letter and the support of the BLLF, Iqbal stormed into the carpet factory. Now having the documentation to prove that bonded labor is against the law, Iqbal demanded freedom for himself and the other children. Finally, after years of enduring torturous conditions, Iqbal and the other children were free! They joyfully raced from the factory, but they left behind furious factory owners.

Iqbal's spirit and courage led him to become an active member of the BLLF. He soon was one of their most famous and respected speakers. Iqbal and Ehsan traveled around the world, educating people about the truths of the carpet industry in Pakistan. They encouraged people to boycott Pakistani carpets until the Pakistani government enforced the Bonded Labor Act. This act would cancel all obligations of bonded laborers to their employers and would set the laborers free.

Iqbal's eloquent speeches and hard work proved to be very effective. Once people heard Iqbal's impassioned description of the terrible conditions of child-labor slavery, they did what they could to support him and his cause. And as a result, the carpet industry suffered greatly. Some Pakistanian companies decided to abide by the Bonded Labor Act, now more strictly enforced by the Pakistani government. The industries that followed the rules were able to put a RUGMARK label on their carpets. To this day this label helps these industries' sales.

While educating people all around the world, Iqbal finally got a formal education. Iqbal went to school, one of the many founded by the BLLF in Pakistan. Attending school felt like a privilege for Iqbal, his friends, and former laborers. A bright and lively student, Iqbal was thrilled to learn how to read and write!

Iqbal continued to be noticed. In 1994, when he was only 12, Iqbal won the Reebok Human Rights Award, which honors people under the age of 30 who have made a big difference in the fight for human rights. Iqbal was the youngest person ever to receive this award. The award helped make people around the world aware of Iqbal's cause.

Unfortunately, this story doesn't have a happy ending. On April 16, 1995, when Iqbal was 13 years old, he visited his family for Easter. He was enjoying the day outside, riding his bike with his cousins when suddenly he was shot and killed. The identity of the person responsible for his murder still remains a mystery. Although the Human Rights Commission of Pakistan led many investigations, the investigators constantly changed their stories about what had really happened. Some believe Iqbal was murdered by the "carpet mafia," people representing the carpet factory owners who disliked the BLLF or Iqbal's working with them.

Despite the short time he had to enjoy his new life, Iqbal took full advantage of one of his rights, his freedom of speech. He used this freedom right up until the end of his life to fight for children's rights, and made a huge difference. Undeterred by personal risk, he showed immense courage in his fight against Pakistan's powerful carpet industry. In the end, Iqbal's eloquence and bravery helped to liberate thousands of child factory workers.

Child labor is still a problem in some parts of the world. If you would like to learn more about child labor or help out, go to: **http://www.amnesty.org** and **http://www.unicef.org/aclabor/explore.htm**

Jacob Dunnack

Jacob Dunnack has always loved to play sports, especially baseball, which he often played when he went to visit his grandparents. Since they didn't have sporting equipment at their home, Jacob would bring his own bat and ball. Sometimes, when he forgot to bring a ball, he and his grandmother would create balls out of crumpled newspapers and masking tape. But this was not an acceptable long-term solution for six-year-old Jacob.

Then he came up with an idea so that he would never again have a bat without a baseball. This clever boy knew that the perfect time to share his idea would be at his school's Invention Convention. Jacob entered a sample of his invention, called the JD Batball, which is a hollow bat in which baseballs could be stored. Jacob's parents helped him create the sample by cutting the top off one of Jacob's own plastic bats. Jacob then put a few balls inside the hollow bat and used a Styrofoam plug to keep the balls from falling out. Everyone loved his invention, and Jacob won first prize!

Now that Jacob knew the widespread appeal of the Batball, he decided to go the next step. He and his parents took the Batball idea to some stores. Jacob explained it as a "baseball bat that opens like luggage." If kids could store and carry baseballs inside their bats, they'd always be prepared to play without searching for a ball or fumbling with too much equipment.

Stores such as Toys "Я" Us were interested in his idea. So Jacob and his family set up a company and hired Cado Company, a manufacturer in Massachusetts, to make the Batball—a plastic, hollow baseball bat with a twist-lock top. Three plastic balls were included that fit easily inside the bat's hollow body. Jacob explained that the three balls represented the three kids in his family. The JD Batball won the National Mail Order Association award, naming it Connecticut's top original product "Made in America" for 2002.

Jacob is very involved in his family's toy company, doing tasks such as picking out the colors for the bats and giving free samples to his friends so that they can test them. He likes having his picture on the package. Jacob explains that his parents are taking care of the business end of the company until he gets a bit older.

For most kids, carrying a bat and baseball separately is annoying but can be easily done. For Jacob, carrying a bat and baseballs separately is extremely difficult because he has physical disabilities—and has had them since he was almost a year old.

Jacob was born with a heart defect, which required him to have many surgeries as a young boy. During one of his operations, at the age of 11 months, Jacob had a stroke. The part of Jacob's brain that was damaged from the stroke left him with limited use of the right side of his body, speaking difficulties, and partial blindness. At one point, Jacob's doctors did not think he was even going to live. But Jacob overcame the odds.

Throughout the years, Jacob's disabilities have made his everyday functioning quite demanding. Although Jacob knows what he wants to say when speaking, it takes him more time to express himself clearly. Jacob also can't easily move the right side of his body, especially his right arm. This makes activities in which he needs to use both arms very challenging, such as carrying a bat and a baseball separately. Jacob has worked very hard in therapy to improve his speech and movement skills.

In addition, Jacob has needed to learn how to deal each day with changes in his eyesight. Sometimes Jacob has "good eye days," seeing things clearly, and other days he has "bad eye days," when things appear blurry. But his vision has improved a great deal over the years. Jacob has learned how to read Braille, which he says is "like a secret code," in case his eyesight ever gets worse again.

Jacob has not only needed to adjust his life to handle his situation but also to handle some kids who tease him. He explains, "I don't care. My friends like me, and I just laugh at the ones who say mean things." Jacob has many friends who feel lucky to have a friend with such "cool ideas." Despite what other kids might think, Jacob feels "normal," knowing that it is normal for people to be different in their own way.

Overall, Jacob is a healthy boy. He doesn't let his physical challenges keep him from doing what he enjoys, like rollerblading, bike riding, playing hockey, and, especially playing baseball. He still goes to a heart doctor every year, but reports that "my heart is strong and healthy. I have a murmur, but it is okay."

Jacob never gives up and focuses on his strengths rather than his weaknesses. For instance, he's got good ideas and is a great problem solver. After all, he's figured out creative ways to make things simpler. Some of his solutions help him alone, but others, like the Batball, make things simpler for everyone who plays baseball.

Jacob spends a lot of time making people aware of heart disease. He speaks at local colleges and schools about proper diet and exercise to help prevent the disease. Jacob often gives JD Batballs to children at the Connecticut Children's Medical Center. He explains, "My toy makes kids happy, and that makes me happy and proud."

This special kid inventor hopes one day to be a firefighter. If Jacob follows his own advice, "Just always be nice to everyone and don't ever give up on anything that you really believe in," he is sure to make his dream into a reality.

Visit Jacob's website, **jacobsportz.com** or e-mail him at Jdbatball@cs.com to learn more about his invention or what to do if you have an invention of your own.

Janine LiCare

*I*n 1993, when Janine LiCare was only three years old, her father suddenly died of a heart attack. Her mother, Jennifer, took Janine, their cat, and a few belongings and bravely set out to start a new life.

The LiCares went around the world looking for an area to live that was both affordable and offered good health benefits. Finally they found what

they needed for a comfortable life in Costa Rica, a small country in Central America. Jennifer, Janine, and their cat settled in a small, quiet town called Manuel Antonio, which is located within a tall rain forest. The rain forest and the wildlife that live within it are found all along a hillside. At the bottom of the hill, the forest ends and meets the flat, white sand beaches along Manuel Antonio's coastline. It is in this part of Manuel Antonio that Janine lives. The weather is warm, and Janine describes it as a place where you can hear monkeys playing outside your door.

Janine and her mother became very comfortable in their community and made some good friends. One of the main reasons they love Manuel Antonio is because of its large national park. The park has acres and acres of rain forest, with all sorts of wildlife, including sloths, monkeys, birds, frogs, and snakes. Janine and her mother visited the park so often that it became a constant part of their lives. Life in the rain forest helped them appreciate and respect their environment.

In 1998 Janine and a friend noticed that many trees from the rain forest were being cut down and learned that the whole rain forest was in danger of being destroyed. Farmers wanted to use the land for cattle grazing, and developers wanted to use it to build buildings. The girls knew that they had to do something to stop it. Cutting down a rain forest kills many trees, some of which are endangered. It also destroys the homes and habitats of many animals, including the endangered titi monkey.

Janine and her friend took immediate action and found a way to raise money to help save the rain forest. With the support of Janine's mother, the girls set up a stand near the street and sold painted rocks and crafts to help spread the word. As they continued to pursue their goal, they learned what needed to be done to save the rain forest and the habitats within it. They also realized that there was a great need to educate others about the importance of saving the rain forest.

About a year later, their roadside stand grew into a non-profit organization called Kids Saving the Rain Forest, often referred to as KSTR. Janine and her friend were just nine years old! In 1999 KSTR members decided on the goals that they hoped to accomplish, such as educating children about the rain forest, preserving local rain forest land, taking care of baby animals, and working toward the survival of the endangered titi monkeys. The girls were constantly looking for new resources to help KSTR raise funds to accomplish these objectives.

KSTR raised $17,000 at that time, half of which was used to purchase about four acres of prime rain forest (bought near the girls' homes). This money was raised through auctions, tag sales, and an adopt-a-tree program. The adopt-a-tree program allows a person to pay $20 to purchase a tree, then have it planted in the rainforest in someone's name.

Today KSTR continues to raise money to pay for the projects needed to help and protect all that live within their land. Many of these projects must be funded each year to maintain the work done. Some of these funds come from the sales in their environmental store, which grew from the girls' tiny roadside stand. It now sells kids' and local artists' work. The girls also illustrated a book called *The Legend of the Blue Monkey*, written by Janine's mom, Jennifer Rice. They make money from the sales of this book, which also helps fund these projects.

One of KSTR's major projects that must be regularly funded is replanting trees on the land. KSTR plants a number of different types of trees that are native to the area to restore the area to the thick forest it was

before. Some of the endangered trees that were cut down are now being replaced.

Many of the trees being replanted are needed for the survival of specific animals in the forest because these trees provide necessary food and shelter for them. The titi monkey is an example of an endangered animal whose natural habitat within the rain forest is disappearing. As specific trees in its habitat disappear, so do the insects that are attracted to these trees. Because insects are a food source for the monkeys, certain trees are now being planted to replace the titi monkey's food source. The planting must be a regular process to make sure that the natural habitats that once existed are built up again and maintained. So far KSTR has planted over 4,500 trees!

Another important KSTR project is the building of "monkey bridges." Rain forest monkeys often cross the roads to go from one part of the rainforest to another. As they do this, they can easily get killed by speeding cars or by touching electrical wires. With fewer than 2,000 titi monkeys remaining, the building of the monkey bridges is needed for the survival of the species. These bridges are built over the roads, connecting one part of the rain forest to another part. The monkeys can then use the bridges to cross over safely. When Janine finishes a big project, like building a monkey bridge, she feels happy. She loves the feeling of attaining a goal.

KSTR also developed a program for saving baby animals. KSTR takes care of sick, injured, or abandoned baby animals and then releases them back into the wild when they are ready. This is an especially meaningful part of the organization for Janine, a true animal lover. She explains, "Pets and animals make me happy because I know that I can trust them and that they are always there for me."

Janine and her organization have done in six years what some people would hope to accomplish in a lifetime! Janine is determined to educate as many people as possible—especially those her own age—about why they should care about the rain forest and how they can help save it. Janine feels it's up to her generation to protect the rain forest, saying, "If we don't make a difference, then who will?" Janine explains that it's as simple as not wasting paper and recycling. Janine is pleased that more and more people are learning about the rain forest because of her ongoing work.

Janine hopes that one day KSTR will become an international organization that saves rain forests all around the world. Now KSTR has grown to include over 250 volunteers worldwide. Janine and her organization don't know if they can save all of the rain forests, but they aim to try.

This amazing 16-year-old has been recognized worldwide for her accomplishments. She was named Person of the Month in the June/July 2002 issue of *Teen Magazine*, *National Geographic Explorer's* "Kid Power Person of the Month" in 2002, International "Amazing Kid" of the Month in April 2003, number one of *Teen Magazine's* Ten Teens Changing the World in 2003, and received the 2004 Young Eco-Hero Award from Action for Nature—to name just of few of the honors she has earned. Here's a piture of Janine (far right), and others involved in KSTR receiving the Costa Rican Bandera Azul Ecological (Ecological Blue Flag) program award. KSTR received this award—founded on the importance of education and informa- tion about the environment and the  protection of nature (including clean beaches)—in 2005 and 2006.

School is a priority for her as well, and Janine is one of the top students in her class. She speaks English and Spanish fluently and is learning French. Social Studies and English are her favorite subjects. Janine hopes to become a lawyer one day.

When Janine isn't working on KSTR or her schoolwork, she describes herself as an ordinary teenager who daydreams about boys, loves musicals such as *Moulin Rouge* and *Chicago,* adores hip-hop music, and enjoys hanging out with her friends. However, Janine does feel at times that she has different goals than other kids her own age.

Janine is an example of how a kid can make a huge difference in the world. She says, "If you truly believe in something and truly want something, you can accomplish it, no matter what other people say." She offers further advice, "Always stick to your beliefs and follow through [with] your ideas."

For more information about Janine's organization, go to **http://www.kidssavingtherainforest.org/**

Joey Davis

*A*s 11-year-old Joey Davis comes home from school each day, his stomach does flip-flops. He is not worried about the grade he got on his math test or how he'll do in his next wrestling match. Instead, he is nervous about walking through his neighborhood to reach home. Joey lives in Compton, California, a section of Los Angeles that has had a reputation for drug, gun, and gang activity. The constant threat of this dangerous area makes every day a struggle. Joey compares the activity in his neighborhood to that of being in the middle of a war.

Despite his fears, Joey has been able to remain strong and focused, staying clear of bad influences. With the help, support, and love of his family, Joey has worked hard and already has achieved a great deal in his young life. He has developed into a talented athlete—he's skilled at track and field and is a champion wrestler and football player.

During the winter wrestling season, Joey practices wrestling five days a week, for a minimum of two hours each day at a nearby high-school gym. His father takes him to wrestling practice every day and is also his coach. Coach Davis, who himself was awarded "Role Model of the Year" in 2003 by the mayor of Compton, teaches his students new moves and special wrestling holds, or positions. Joey does many different drills to sharpen these skills and also works on his endurance by jogging and sprinting.

All of this hard work has paid off. Joey has won over 120 wrestling matches. He's earned six consecutive California State Championship titles, the Triple Crown in California, and the California Legislative Award. In 2002, when Joey was eight years old, he finished third in the world and second in the state among 9–12 year olds. He was runner-up for the world

championship in 2003 and 2004 and won the world title in 2005!

Joey first became interested in wrestling when, at age six, he saw his dad coach his older brother's high-school wrestling team. Joey has a special memory of seeing his brother in a match and watching the referee raise his brother's hand in victory. Joey says, "I liked what I saw!" This image of his brother, along with Joey's natural athletic ability, inspired him to try wrestling. Today, when it's Joey who wins a wrestling match, he explains that he feels "great, very happy, satisfied, and proud."

Joey also plays football for the Snoop Dogg All Stars, a semipro team of 9–12 year olds financed by the rapper Snoop Dog. In 2005 Joey and his Snoop Dogg All Star teammates beat the Jacksonville Jaguars to win the "Snooper Bowl" (a scaled-down form of the Super Bowl for kids).

When Joey is not practicing his sports, he likes to hang out with his friends and play video games. He also likes to ride his scooter, watch professional wrestling and football on TV, listen to rap music, and eat pizza. Joey enjoys school, where his favorite subject is math.

His goals are to become a high-school wrestling champion and to play pro football in the NFL (National Football League). With Joey's focus and talent, and strong family support, it would be no surprise to see him one day tearing up the gridiron on TV. You may have already seen him on UPN's *Eve* show, MTV, VH1, or as the July 2003 "Amazing Kid."

Joey feels lucky to have a supportive father and a family that "loves him, cheers for him, and gives him good luck." Despite the difficult odds Joey faces, he finds the strength within himself and his strong support system to help him stay on a successful path.

If you would like to contact Joey or his family, please e-mail them at: moedawg140@hotmail.com.

Shay Desfrosiers

The cultures of most societies have changed over time and continue to adjust to the world around them. Changes can be seen in many areas, such as in skills, dress, arts, education, tools, and ways of life. Many societies take great pride in their heritage, which tells a lot about its people and what makes them unique.

Shay Desfrosiers is a Native American girl whose heritage is very much part of her life. She lives in Browns Valley, Minnesota, on an Indian reservation. The reservation where Shay lives is called the Sisseton-Wahpeton and is the home of many people from the Dakota tribe. Her parents come from two Native American tribes—her mother is Dakota, and her father is Ojibwa. Shay speaks English but also knows both the Dakota and Ojibwa languages. Her Ojibwa Indian name is WE ZAW GO'NE BIIK, meaning "Golden Eagle Woman."

Shay's heritage comes from both her mother's and father's tribes. She learns about her heritage from her tribal school and from her family, through oral tradition. Shay loves to hear the stories that have been passed down from her ancestors, describing how things came to be. One of her favorites is about the origin of the drum, which was told to her by her father. In the story, a famous chief was told to find four spirits in order to help his tribe survive. He found the spirits singing and dancing around a drum. The spirits told the chief to take the drum back to his tribe and to let it guide them to good fortune. He listened to the spirits, took the drum, and his tribe did well. Someday Shay will tell this story to her children, who will then tell it to their children, and so it will continue for future generations.

Shay and her family are very spiritual. Her heroes include, "all the animal clans who protect us spiritually in our culture." Shay is "very proud of being a Native American." She respects her people's heritage and likes to share her culture to help do away with untrue stories about Native Americans. Shay says, "It makes me feel weird to think that some people believe we still live in teepees and ride horses and hunt buffalo!"

Shay is a typical kid in many respects. She likes school and reading, playing on her computer, practicing her cheerleading, and hanging out with her friends. But one way she is different from many other children is in the great joy she takes in powwow dancing.

A powwow is a get-together of Native Americans where there is often dancing and singing to celebrate life. It typically lasts about four days, from Thursday to Sunday. Since powwows are usually held outside, they take place during the summer months. Her father explains, "Shay was born with a gift to powwow dance...and has been dancing ever since she could walk!" Shay says that she learned to dance by "watching the other dancers dance and getting encouraged by my mom."

There is a powwow circuit, where different tribes organize and host the powwows. Some are "contest powwows" in which different tribes compete, and others are "contemporary powwows" in which tribes celebrate life and special occasions like births, weddings, and graduations. Shay enters powwow competitions. When she was eight years old, she competed in Seattle, Washington, with some of her friends. They won first place and got trophies and special jackets. That was a memorable day for her.

Shay is known throughout the powwow circuit because she is so young and has won many competitions in places like Seattle, Washington; Oklahoma City, Oklahoma; and California. Shay has even been "adopted" by other tribes, such as the Kiowa. That means that their tribal leaders have given her the right to dance in their styles, which is considered a great honor.

In addition to dancing at powwows, Shay sometimes accompanies or dances with her parents' dance group. Shay's parents are members of the Lakota Indian Dance Theatre. This is a traveling dance group that goes around the world performing traditional dances. The goal of the group is not only to entertain, but also to teach the culture and traditions of different Native American Tribes. At the age of six, Shay became the youngest person to perform with the group. She travels and at times performs with them in places from New York City—at the Museum of Natural History—to schools in California. Shay feels "happy and proud" when she dances for others, and she enjoys sharing her culture.

Shay's mother makes the costumes for the family. The costumes are different depending on the dance. For the *Southern Buckskin,* a Kiowa traditional dance, Shay wears an outfit made of buckskin with lots of beadwork. For a sacred Ojibwa dance called the *Jingle,* she wears an outfit made of tin lids shaped into cones, which make a jingling sound when she dances.

Shay is very close to her family and feels happy that powwow dancing keeps them together. She considers herself very lucky to have such excellent role models in her parents because she realizes that not all kids on the reservation have parents who are as involved in their lives. She has some advice for kids: "Be alcohol and drug free and finish school!" Shay has embraced her heritage and family values, making them an integral part of her life.

Nibia Pastrana Santiago

On the warm and balmy island of Puerto Rico lives a graceful teenaged dancer named Nibia Pastrana. Nibia lives with her parents and younger brother in the town of Aguas Buenas. She attended Colegio Bautista de Caguas, where she especially enjoyed history and science classes. But her true passion, without a doubt, is her dancing. She hopes one day to develop into a great flamenco dancer and own a dance academy.

Nibia has always loved to dance. Her family remembers her as a little girl constantly feeling the rhythm of any sound around her and moving her body to all music. Her love for rhythms and sounds still remains.

Nibia explains, "Music is in my veins…I was born to dance." She dances to free herself. "It's a way to express my feelings, my thoughts, my ideas, and of course to be me." Nibia says, "When I dance, my body becomes an instrument, and for me, every movement feels like writing poetry. Dancing is an opportunity to create and be part of your creation."

Nibia knows many different kinds of dance, such as ballet, modern dance, and salsa, which is popular in Puerto Rico. She does dance moves that have African-Caribbean roots like bomba, hip-hop, and flamenco, and has learned the basics of belly dancing.

Nibia wanted to do more than just practice her own dance routines and moves. She wanted to find a way to combine her love of dance with her love of people. Nibia has been able to do this through Danza Libre, a dance group that she founded with the help of Girl Scouts of the USA.

Nibia developed Danza Libre with a goal in mind. She focused on girls living in a public-housing unit in Puerto Rico. Many of these girls come from dangerous neighborhoods or difficult backgrounds. They usually do not have much family support. These girls have very low self-esteem and often make unhealthy choices. Nibia wanted to provide these girls with a positive focus and something to believe in. Because Nibia believes that everyone can enjoy the arts, she invited these girls to join Danza Libre. Her program provided them with physical conditioning and other healthy choices. It helped them stick with a project and learn new ways to do things. And most important, the dance workshops gave these girls more pride and trust in themselves. It helped them work as a team, respect one another, and be more open to expressing their feelings and thoughts.

Through Danza Libre, Nibia was able to take a diverse group of girls and have them dancing, smiling, and feeling good about themselves. Nibia's dance group performs for cultural community events.

Nibia has truly made a difference in these girls' lives. She feels great about working with them and knows she has helped them in so many ways. She says, "It makes me feel special, because the girls let me know how important I am for them. I feel like a cool mom or an older sister for them. For me, it's an honor to be part of their lives and to be a role model for them."

Nibia has been with the Girl Scouts for 11 years and is now a Senior Girl Scout. Through her work with Girl Scouts of the USA, the knowledge she gained from the group, and her sheer determination, she made her goal of Danza Libre into a reality. Her enthusiasm and efforts helped her to get the funding necessary to get her program off the ground. She wrote many letters asking for donations to run the workshops. Nibia believes that being a "friendly and social person" was probably helpful, too.

Besides raising money, Nibia made appointments with people from government agencies that put her in touch with the girls of the public-housing unit. She got to know 18 "wonderful" girls between the ages of eight and 13 who joined Danza Libre.

Nibia's efforts have been highly praised. Because of Danza Libre's amazing success, Nibia was awarded a Girl Scout Gold Award Young Women of Distinction in 2003. This is the highest honor in Girl Scouting. It recognizes Nibia's outstanding success in leadership, community service, career planning, and personal development.

Although the community center where Danza Libre met has been torn down, the girls have not stopped dancing. They continue to dance in different groups and perform often. These girls feel like friends to Nibia and are a source of pride and growth for her.

If you are interested in learning more about Girl Scouts, go to **www.girlscouts.org** or call 1-800-GSUSA-4U.

Sai Gunturi

How do you spell *champion*? S-a-i G-u-n-t-u-r-i. Sai Gunturi is a champion speller and the 2003 winner of the 76th Scripps National Spelling Bee competition.

Spelling comes naturally to this Texas boy. But it was watching his big sister preparing for her spelling bees that first interested Sai in competing. His sister competed in fifth grade and got to Regionals and then made it to the Nationals in seventh grade. When Sai won first place in his school's third-grade spelling bee, he decided to commit himself to preparing for regional and national spelling bees.

Sai began competing in Regionals and did so well that he qualified for the Scripps National Spelling Bee, probably the most well-known of all spelling bees. In May 2000, ten-year-old Sai competed in this event and came in 32nd. In 2001 he was 16th, and in 2002 he tied for seventh. Sai decided that his goal for the 76th Scripps National Spelling Bee in 2003 was to rank even higher, something he did each year he competed.

The Scripps National Spelling Bee is set up in rounds. With each round, some students are eliminated. The rounds continue until only one speller remains. Studying words from the dictionary every day was enough to prepare Sai for the beginning rounds of the Nationals. But it's more difficult to prepare for the final rounds because many of the spelling words can't be found in a regular dictionary. Instead contestants must look in the most complete and largest American dictionary, *Webster's Third New International Dictionary,* and its Addenda Section, which together contain more than 470,000 words.

Sai explains that even after studying regularly for four years, it's impossible to memorize every word in the dictionary. So in the end, you're either given a word you don't know or are lucky enough to get a word you do know. Sai just decided that he would do his best to become familiar with as many words as he could, using his strong visual memory. "When I study a word, it usually registers in my mind as a sort of picture. So whenever I hear a word, the word just kind of pops into my head as a picture again, and it's just like reading it."

Sai's mom and sister helped him to practice. They asked him a word, and then he would try to spell it. They also made flashcards. Sai explained that reviewing the definition, or giving meaning to the word, helped him remember it.

During the bee the pronouncer (the person who gives the student a word to spell) not only pronounces the word correctly, but answers any of the speller's questions about the word's pronunciation, definition, use in a sentence, and history. This extra information might either spark memories of a familiar word or helps the speller figure out an unfamiliar word.

The ESPN sports network, which televised the 76th Scripps National Spelling Bee, decided to learn more about the students competing in spelling bees. ESPN picked four students in regional spelling bees who were likely champions. They filmed these students during the early stages of qualifying for the Nationals to watch them prepare and learn what their daily lives were like. Sai was one of the students chosen. It was the first time something like that had ever happened to him. He felt proud, but it was a bit strange for him, too, because for weeks he was surrounded by cameras and microphones. Of the experience, Sai reports that it was "pretty cool but also got kind of annoying because there were people following me around all of the time."

Sai's family accompanied him to Washington, D.C., where the 76th Scripps National Spelling Bee competition was held. Sai was among the 251 finalists. Spellers ranged from 8–15 years old and were almost evenly divided between boys and girls. Sai knew many of the students from earlier contests.

Round One of the 76th Bee began with each finalist being given one word to spell orally. One hundred seventy-five students went on to Round Two. In Round Two, students took a 25-word written exam. Students who missed 11 words or more were eliminated. Sai was one of 84 finalists who advanced to the following rounds, which would be televised live the next day.

The next morning the finalists sat together waiting their turns. Each student would have to spell a word correctly in order to advance to the next round. Each time his turn arrived to step up to the microphone, Sai felt his heart beat quickly in anticipation. But once he heard the word, his heart slowed down. Sai continued this way until he reached his goal—he had beaten his past record of seventh place! Sai became much calmer in the following rounds.

Sai might have reached his personal goal, but he was far from finished in this bee. He continued to spell his words correctly and finally found himself competing with only one other student, Evelyn Blacklock from Tuxedo Park, New York. Sai didn't even feel nervous, explaining that it would be a win-win situation. "If I lost, I did better than last time, and if I won the spelling bee, that would [be] super awesome."

In the 14th round, after Sai had spelled his word, *rhathymia* correctly, Evelyn misspelled her word, *gnathonic*. She spelled it *nathonic* (the *g* is silent). Now it was the 15th round and Sai's turn. He realized that because Evelyn had just misspelled a word, he could actually win if he spelled his next word correctly. Sai described what he was thinking and feeling at that moment "...I can win but it's just as cool if I don't. So [I] had a little lurch in my stomach, kind of like the type that you get right before going on a roller coaster, but that was it."

During the earlier rounds, Sai was able to spell many words correctly, such as *marmoraceous, mistassini, solfeggio, voussoir, halogeton, dipnoous,* and *peirastic*. But would he be able to spell this next word? Sai explained that the audience became so nervous, wondering the same thing. He was given the word *pococurante*. And he spelled it p-o-c-o-c-u-r-a-n-t-e. Correct!

The meaning of *pococurante*—caring little or feeling indifferent—was the opposite of how the people in the audience felt. Sai described that after he spelled it correctly, there was a huge sigh of relief in the room, as if air were being let out of an overblown balloon. Sai was smiling and "kind of laughing" as this happened. He then added, "Although the release of tension in the room was pretty high, you could say that my tension release was essentially four years' worth of tension going *sssssssssssss* out of the room." And then the audience cheered. Sai realized he had just won!

"Wow, I got what I've been working on for four years," he remarked, but then added, "It just so happened that I got the words I knew." But it was his studying for four years that allowed him to know all those words! Sai explained that after winning, it was kind of a "weird feeling. You're happy, but at the same time, the adrenaline you've been running on just kind of slows down, so you feel really drained."

Sai received a $12,000 cash prize, an engraved trophy and reference books from Merriam-Webster and Encyclopaedia Britannica, among other prizes. To celebrate his victory, his family ordered pizza in their hotel room, and they watched the Dallas Mavericks vs. San Antonio Spurs basketball game. This was exactly how Sai wanted to celebrate. He had been so busy that it was the perfect way to wind down.

Sai explained, "I really didn't realize the enormity of it all...I actually woke up the night after I won, around midnight, and woke up my sister and asked whether I had won or whether I had just hallucinated it all because I was working too hard." She confirmed that he had indeed won.

Because Sai won, he can no longer compete in the Scripps National Spelling Bee. But he has plenty to keep him busy. Besides his schoolwork,

Sai plays video and computer games. He also likes to relax, sleep, and eat Indian food. Sai hopes one day to pursue a career in medicine as a genetic engineer.

Sai gets his drive to excel from his parents, who are his heroes. His younger brother, who competed in the Regionals, seems to be following Sai. Sai has some advice for kids—after working hard to finally reach the goal that he set in the second grade. He strongly encourages them to "stick with whatever you want to do; don't give up." Sai Gunturi is certainly an i-n-s-p-i-r-a-t-i-o-n!

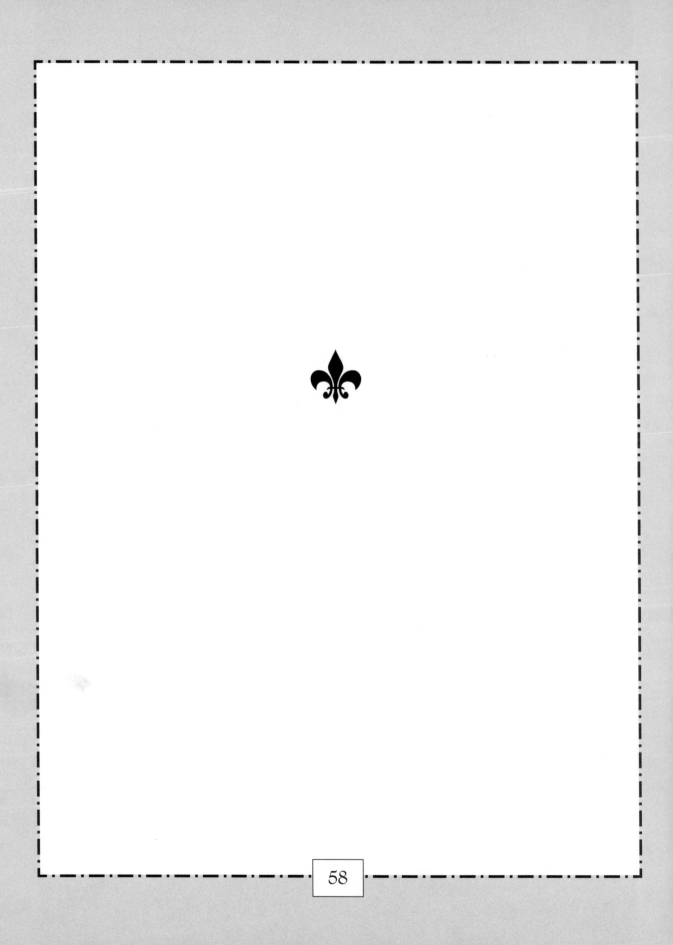

Glossary

ancestors	long line of past relatives
Beijing's Forbidden City	the world's largest palace complex. This small city in the center of the Beijing was once the home of emperors during 1420–1912. Now it is shown as a Palace Museum and a great tourist attraction.
bonded child labor	children held as slaves and made to work as payment for a debt
Bonded Labor Act	law that forbids forced or bonded child labor
Bonded Labor Liberation Front (The BLLF)	an organization founded by Ehsan Ulla Khan to help free children from bonded labor
captive-child syndrome	group of health problems, such as starvation, having twisted bodies, and problems breathing that has killed many of Pakistan's working children by age 12
child labor	forcing children—without a choice or any rights—to spend their days working in unhealthy and cruel conditions, and keeping them from getting an education. Child labor is against the law in most parts of the world.
children's rights laws	laws protecting the rights of children, enforced by the government. No one can take these rights away.

culture	a way of life shaped by heritage that tells a lot about certain people and what makes them unique
endangered	anyone or anything whose ability to continue living is threatened
forms	competition in which martial artists show their ability to perform karate moves with accurate style
Helping Hand	a tool with a magnetic palm and fingers placed at the end of an antenna-like rod that helps to pick up hard-to-reach metal items. Carlos Pena is its inventor.
heritage	customs, ideas, behaviors, and beliefs of a person or group of people passed down from generation to generation, often by word of mouth
JD Batball	a hollow bat in which baseballs can be stored. Jacob Dunnack is the inventor.
motivational speaker	a speaker who persuades others to develop positive behaviors and motivates them to do productive things with their lives
oral tradition	stories that are passed down from generation to generation by word of mouth. It's one way people learn about their heritage, and it is part of their social and cultural life.
Ping-Pong	a popular sport in China, also called *table tennis*. It is like a miniature version of tennis in which a ball is hit with paddles, back and forth over a net set up across a table.

powwow	a get-together of Native Americans where there is dancing and singing to celebrate life
pronouncer	person who gives the word to be spelled to a contestant during a spelling bee. This person not only pronounces the word correctly, but also answers the speller's questions about the word's pronunciation, definition, use in a sentence, and history.
rain forest	wet, steamy, tropical uplands and lowlands near the equator where many endangered animals and plants live
Reebok Human Rights Award	an award that honors people under the age of 30 who have made a big difference in the fight for human rights. This honor helps make people around the world aware of the winner's cause and encourages them to support it. Iqbal Masih won it in 1994.
RUGMARK label	a label carpet industries are able to put on their carpets if they follow the rules of the Bonded Labor Act and use no child labor. Earning this label helps these industries' sales.
sickle cell anemia	a blood disease that affects mainly (but not only) blacks. Someone with sickle cell anemia has deformed red blood cells that cannot carry oxygen around the body efficiently.
sparring	competition in which martial artists gesture karate moves against their opponent with great attention to form

stroke   a sudden attack that occurs when blood, bringing oxygen and nutrients to the brain, can't get to part of the brain. Without receiving oxygen, the cells of this part of the brain die. Therefore, the body parts controlled by these cells no longer work properly.

tribe   a Native American group that shares common ancestors, customs, and laws, and usually lives together in the same community

To my pooh bear, Natalie Jane

—C.R.

For information contact:
MONDO Publishing 980 Avenue of the Americas, New York, NY 10018
Visit our website at http://www.mondopub.com
Printed in U.S.A.

07 08 09 10 11 9 8 7 6 5 4 3 2 1
ISBN 1-59336-324-9

Designed by Jean Cohn

Library of Congress Cataloging-in-Publication Data
Raff, Courtney Granet.   Kids you ought to know / by Courtney Granet Raff.   p. cm.
ISBN 1-59336-324-9   1.   Exceptional children--Case studies 2.   Success in children—
Case studies.   I. Title.   HQ773.5.R34 2006   305.23092'2--dc22   2005037401

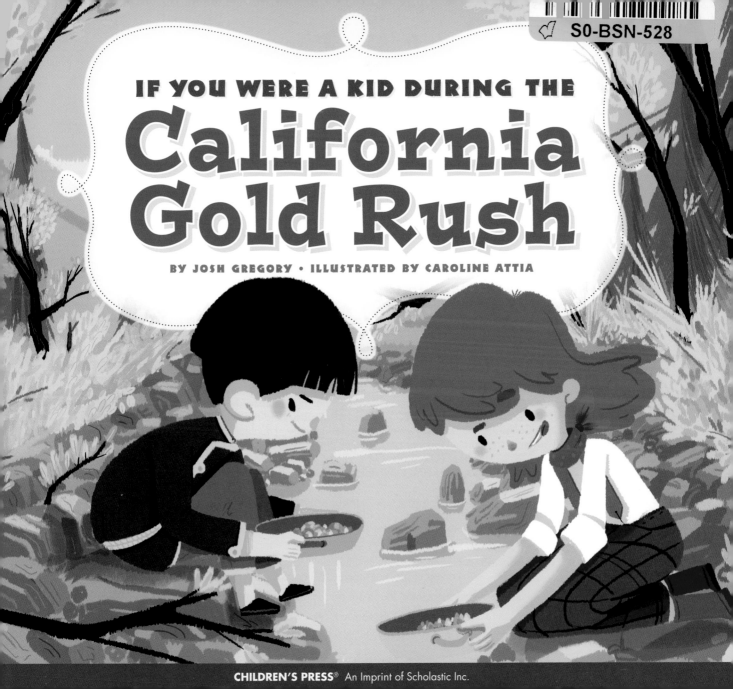

IF YOU WERE A KID DURING THE
California
Gold Rush

BY JOSH GREGORY • ILLUSTRATED BY CAROLINE ATTIA

CHILDREN'S PRESS® An Imprint of Scholastic Inc.

Content Consultant
James Marten, PhD, Professor and Chair, History Department, Marquette University, Milwaukee, Wisconsin

NOTE TO THE READER, PARENT, LIBRARIAN, AND TEACHER: This book combines a historical fiction narrative with nonfiction fact boxes. While all the nonfiction fact boxes are historically accurate and true, the fiction comes solely from the imaginations of the author and illustrator.

Photos ©: 9: Radu Bercan/Shutterstock; 11: Fotosearch/Getty Images; 13: Maryann Preisinger/Dreamstime; 15: The Granger Collection; 17 left: belka_35/iStockphoto; 17 center: Warren_Price/iStockphoto; 17 right: Janet Faye Hastings/Shutterstock; 19: Science History Images/Alamy Images; 21: Bettmann/Getty Images; 23: John Elk III/Alamy Images; 25: The Granger Collection; 27: Herbert Gehr/The LIFE Picture Collection/Getty Images.

Library of Congress Cataloging-in-Publication Data
Names: Gregory, Josh, author. | Attia, Caroline, illustrator.
Title: If you were a kid during the California Gold Rush / by Josh Gregory ; illustrated by Caroline Attia.
Description: New York : Children's Press, an imprint of Scholastic Inc., [2018] | Series: If you were a kid | Includes bibliographical references and index.
Identifiers: LCCN 2017032485 | ISBN 9780531232149 (library binding) | ISBN 9780531243121 (pbk.)
Subjects: LCSH: California—Gold discoveries—Juvenile literature. | California—History—1846-1850—Juvenile literature. | Frontier and pioneer life—California—Juvenile literature.
Classification: LCC F865 .G745 2018 | DDC 979.4/04—dc23
LC record available at https://lccn.loc.gov/2017032485

SCHOLASTIC, CHILDREN'S PRESS, and associated logos are trademarks and/or registered trademarks of Scholastic Inc.

Scholastic Inc., 557 Broadway, New York, NY 10012

1 2 3 4 5 6 7 8 9 10 R 27 26 25 24 23 22 21 20 19 18

TABLE OF CONTENTS

4

A Different Way of Life

On January 24, 1848, a carpenter named James Marshall was working to build a **sawmill** on California's American River. He noticed something sparkling in the water and soon realized that it was gold! News of Marshall's discovery spread through newspapers and word of mouth. This kicked off an era known as the Gold Rush. Thousands of people from around the world hurried to California. They hoped to get rich by finding gold. Most were men who left their families behind in a race to gather gold as quickly as they could. As the Gold Rush went on, many of the **prospectors**' families traveled to California to join them.

Turn the page to set off on your own Gold Rush adventure! You will see that life today is a lot different than it was in the past.

Meet Louise!

Louise Cooper and her mother have recently moved from Illinois to a mining town in California. They came to be with Louise's father and older brother, who have been prospecting for gold. The two men had done well during their first few weeks in California. They sometimes made hundreds of dollars in a single day. Unfortunately, they have not been finding as much gold lately. Food is expensive. Their money is running out. Louise is still hopeful, but things are getting tough for the family . . .

6

Meet Feng!

Li Feng came to California with his father and uncle all the way from China. They sailed more than 5,000 miles (8,047 kilometers) across the Pacific Ocean to get there. Like others, they originally planned to make it rich as gold prospectors. But instead, they have had greater success selling supplies to miners. Feng still wants to look for gold, though. He thinks the chance of getting rich quick is way more exciting than helping to run the family business . . .

"Isn't there anything left to eat?" Louise asked. Her stomach was still growling after her very small breakfast.

"Sorry," her mom answered. "We have to save the rest for later in case your father and brother don't find any gold today. We don't have any money left to buy more food."

Louise sighed. She thought the move to California would make her family rich. But so far, it wasn't working.

8

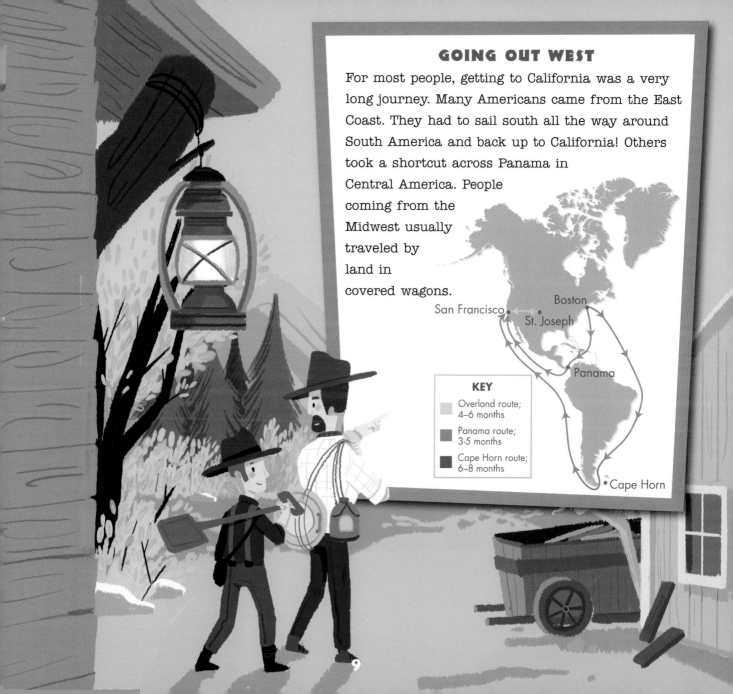

GOING OUT WEST

For most people, getting to California was a very long journey. Many Americans came from the East Coast. They had to sail south all the way around South America and back up to California! Others took a shortcut across Panama in Central America. People coming from the Midwest usually traveled by land in covered wagons.

Boston

San Francisco • St. Joseph

Panama

KEY
Overland route; 4–6 months
Panama route; 3-5 months
Cape Horn route; 6–8 months

• Cape Horn

9

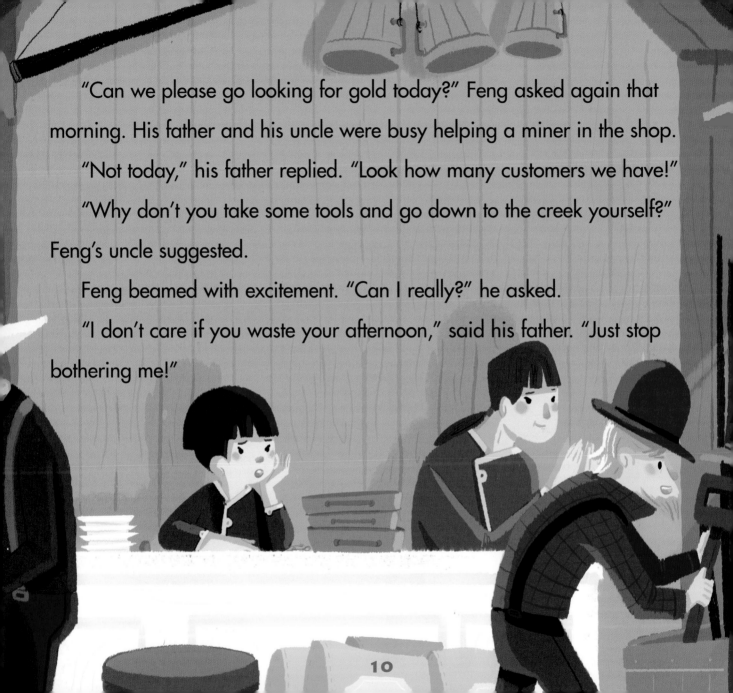

"Can we please go looking for gold today?" Feng asked again that morning. His father and his uncle were busy helping a miner in the shop.

"Not today," his father replied. "Look how many customers we have!"

"Why don't you take some tools and go down to the creek yourself?" Feng's uncle suggested.

Feng beamed with excitement. "Can I really?" he asked.

"I don't care if you waste your afternoon," said his father. "Just stop bothering me!"

10

BUILDING A BUSINESS

Not everyone who traveled to California during the Gold Rush became a miner. The area's population was growing, and businesses were needed to serve everyone. Some of California's new residents found great success selling supplies to miners. Some opened restaurants. Many of these business owners made more money than the average prospector.

Levi Strauss came to San Francisco in 1853 and later became famous by manufacturing and selling the first metal-riveted denim jeans. Here, two gold miners wear Levi's jeans in 1882.

BLUE EYES MINE

Later that morning, Louise was watching her dad and brother pan for gold. She had expected it to be fun and exciting. But after coming to California, she had learned that it was hard, boring work. Worst of all, they hadn't found a single bit of gold all morning.

"I'm going for a walk in the woods," Louise announced.

"Sure, sure," her dad mumbled, without looking up from his work. "Be sure you're back by dinnertime."

TOOLS OF THE TRADE

Prospectors used many tools and **techniques** to collect gold. The simplest way was called panning. A miner would collect water, gravel, and soil from a river or creek in a pan. He would then swirl the pan so the water and other materials would spill over the sides. That would leave the heavier gold at the bottom. A miner might repeat this process up to 50 times each day. And he might only get a little bit of gold. Another common method involved setting up a box by the river or creek. It would be filled with water and materials. Then it was rocked back and forth to separate out the gold.

Miners used pickaxes to break apart rocks and soil as they worked.

"Good luck!" Feng's uncle said with a chuckle. "You're going to need it. Look how many people are out looking for gold. None of them are getting rich."

"I know," Feng answered. "But I'm bored of working here every day." He placed a pan and some snacks in a bag and headed out the door. His uncle shrugged and shook his head.

COMING TO AMERICA

During the Gold Rush, many **immigrants** came to California in hopes of getting rich. People from China joined the Gold Rush in especially large numbers. In 1849, there were 54 Chinese people living in California. By 1876, there were 116,000!

Chinese children walk through San Francisco's Chinatown sometime around 1900.

Louise was walking through the woods. Suddenly, she heard a noise in front of her. A boy popped out from behind a tree. She jumped back, surprised.

"Hi," the boy said. "I'm Feng!"

"You scared me!" Louise exclaimed.

She introduced herself, and the two decided to look for gold together. Soon, they came to a creek. Feng offered to share his snacks with Louise. She was very grateful for something to eat. Afterward, she bent down to drink from the creek.

"There's something sparkling here!" she yelled. "I think I found gold!"

WHAT'S FOR LUNCH?

During the Gold Rush, most people relied on simple meals. The meals needed to be prepared and eaten quickly. People did not want to take long breaks from looking for gold. Sourdough bread was very popular. Some miners purchased foods such as bacon and beans from stores. Others hunted wild animals for meat. Fruits and vegetables were very hard to come by. This caused many people to come down with **scurvy**.

"I can't believe it!" Louise said. "My family is going to be so excited."

"Quiet!" Feng warned. "If other miners hear, they'll show up. Then they'll take all the gold for themselves."

Louise promised to be more careful. The two friends collected as much gold as they could with Feng's tools. But it was getting dark. They split up their shares and agreed to meet at Feng's the next day.

A DIFFICULT LIFE

Mining for gold was hard, dangerous work. All kinds of injuries were common, from cuts to broken bones. There were often no doctors around to help wounded miners. Disease was another big problem. More than half of all miners were **infected** with hookworms. These worms dug into the feet of people with worn-out boots. Some people had no boots at all. Miners also got sick from drinking unclean water. People tended to live very close to one another and had poor **hygiene**. Sicknesses spread easily among them.

Miners got dirty, sweaty, and wet as they worked all day.

Louise couldn't wait to show her family her gold. They stared in surprise as she revealed it.

"We're saved!" her mom exclaimed.

Everyone started discussing plans to gather more gold at Louise's spot the next day.

"Don't forget about Feng," Louise said. "It's his gold, too."

Thinking hard, her dad rubbed his chin. "Well," he said, "I guess that's true."

HOME SWEET HOME

When the Gold Rush began, newly arrived miners had nowhere to live. They often slept outdoors or in quickly built shacks. Over time, these early camps grew to become towns. People built houses, stores, and other buildings. Some even built simple hotels where miners could pay to sleep in a bed. But these buildings were far from fancy. People often had to deal with leaky roofs, rats, and other problems.

Mining camps often became bustling towns full of people and activity.

Feng got up early the next morning
and started gathering his tools.

"Where are you going?" his father asked. "You had
your fun yesterday. Today, you need to stay and work."

Slowly, Feng pulled a handkerchief from his pocket
and unwrapped it.

"Is that what I think it is?" his father asked.

Feng nodded. "I know where to get more, too."

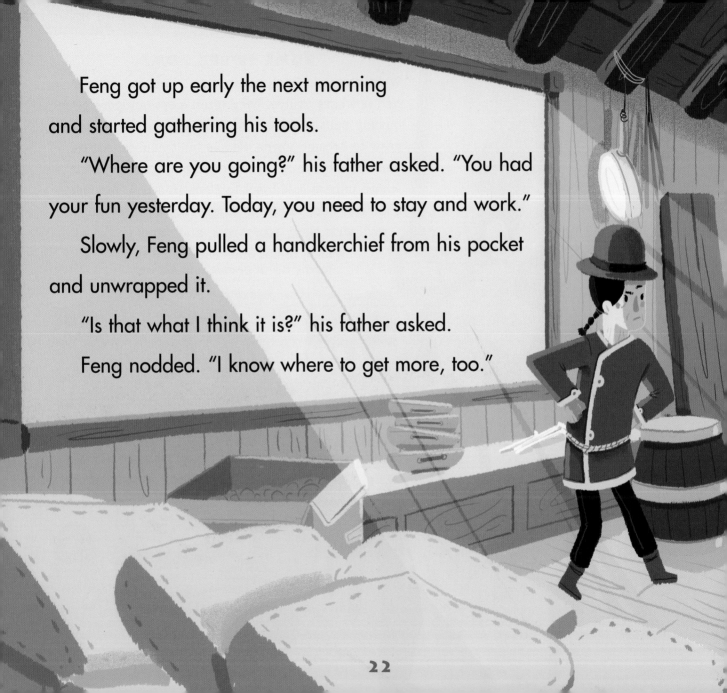

AN $80 EGG?

As the Gold Rush went on, supplies started to become very expensive. There were few farms in California. Food had to be brought in from other states. But too many people were moving to California. There wasn't enough food to go around. Merchants raised their prices as high as they could. A single egg could cost $3 in 1851. That would be more than $80 in today's money!

Stores in gold rush towns sold everything from food to mining tools.

Just then, Louise arrived at the store with her dad and brother. Feng's father demanded that they show him where the gold was. Louise's father refused. The adults started arguing about who had a right to the gold.

"Stop!" yelled Louise. "There's plenty for all of us."

"Yeah," said Feng as he pointed out the window. "And people are starting to pay attention to all the shouting."

With that, everyone got much quieter. They started planning how to collect the gold together.

THE ORIGINAL CALIFORNIANS

Prospectors were not the first people to come to California. When the Gold Rush began, Native Americans had been living in the area for a long time. Prospectors and other settlers took control of the Native Americans' land. They either killed the natives, forced them to leave, or made them work. Between 1845 and 1870, California's Native American population went from 150,000 to 30,000.

California's Native Americans suffered greatly as a result of the Gold Rush.

They needed to stop other miners from following them. So everyone took different paths to the gold. Louise's dad and brother were experienced miners. Feng's family had the latest tools. They worked all day and collected more gold than they could have imagined.

"This is amazing," said Louise's dad. "We're going to have so much money from this gold. You can have seconds at breakfast every day now, Louise!"

"Just wait," said Louise. "You haven't seen anything yet."

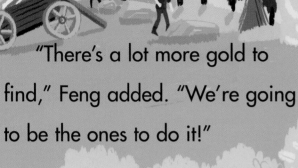

"There's a lot more gold to find," Feng added. "We're going to be the ones to do it!"

THE END OF AN ERA

By the end of the 1850s, prospectors had found most of the gold that was easy to reach. More gold was buried deeper underground. Collecting that gold required powerful **hydraulic** equipment. Individual gold miners were not able to do this kind of work. They were soon replaced by large mining companies. It was the end of an era.

California gold miners relied more and more on heavy machinery in the decades following the Gold Rush.

California During the Gold Rush

During the Gold Rush, cities such as San Francisco and Sacramento grew rapidly as miners flooded into the region. Most gold discoveries took place in the area between the Sierra Nevada mountains along California's eastern border and the Sacramento and San Joaquin Rivers.

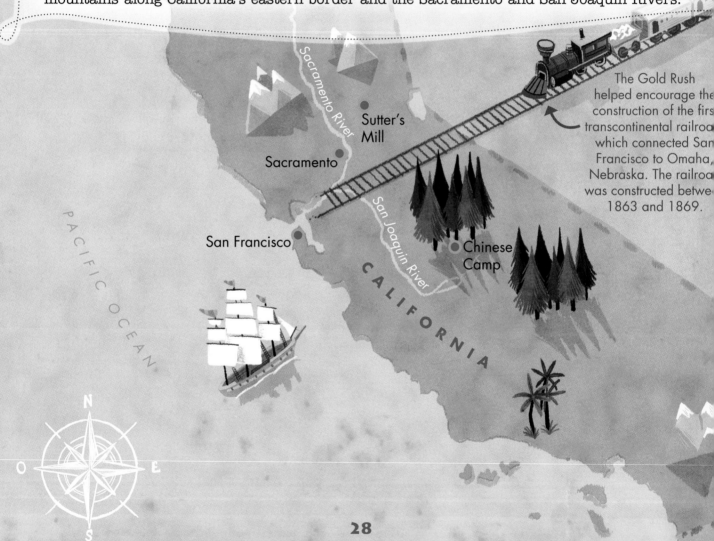

The Gold Rush helped encourage the construction of the first transcontinental railroad which connected San Francisco to Omaha, Nebraska. The railroad was constructed between 1863 and 1869.

Sacramento River

Sutter's Mill

Sacramento

San Joaquin River

San Francisco

Chinese Camp

PACIFIC OCEAN

CALIFORNIA

Timeline

1846 The Native American population of California is about 150,000. The non-native population is about 7,600 to 8,000.

January 24, 1848 The Gold Rush kicks off when a man named James Marshall discovers gold at Sutter's Mill.

February 2, 1848 The United States takes control of California after a war with Mexico.

April 1, 1848 Newspapers are sent out from California announcing the gold discovery.

September 9, 1850 California becomes the 31st state.

1852 At the peak of the Gold Rush, about $80 million worth of gold is collected in California. This would be worth about $2 billion in today's money.

1860 At the conclusion of the Gold Rush, California's official state population is about 380,000.

1870 California's Native American population has dropped to about 30,000.

Words to Know

hydraulic (hye-DRAW-lik) describing machines that work on power created by liquid moving through pipes under pressure

hygiene (HYE-jeen) the practice of keeping yourself and the things around you clean in order to stay healthy

immigrants (IM-i-gruhnts) people who move from one country to another and settle there

infected (in-FEKT-id) carrying germs or viruses that cause disease

prospectors (PRAH-spek-turz) people who are in search of something, such as gold

sawmill (SAW-mil) a place where people use machines to saw logs into lumber

scurvy (SKUR-vee) a disease caused by a lack of vitamin C

techniques (tek-NEEKS) ways of doing something that require skill

Index

ABOUT THE AUTHOR

Josh Gregory is the author of more than 120 books for kids. He has written about everything from animals to technology to history. A graduate of the University of Missouri–Columbia, he currently lives in Chicago, Illinois.

ABOUT THE ILLUSTRATOR

Caroline Attia is an award-winning illustrator and animator. She graduated from the École nationale supérieure des Arts Décoratifs (ENSAD) in Paris, where she directed her first short film, *Tango on Saw*. She works from her studio in Montreuil, France.

Visit this Scholastic website for more information about the California Gold Rush:

www.factsfornow.scholastic.com
Enter the keywords **Gold Rush**

32